Y0-CCZ-005

PASSPORT'S

TRIP
PLANNER
& TRAVEL
DIARY

PASSPORT BOOKS
a division of *NTC Publishing Group*
Lincolnwood, Illinois USA

PERSONAL INFORMATION

Name

Home Address

Home telephone

Drivers license number

International drivers license number

Passport number

Traveler's check numbers

Medical Information

Blood type

Allergies

Doctor

Telephone

In case of emergency, please contact:

Name

Address

Telephone

Published by Passport Books, a division of NTC Publishing Group.
©1991 by NTC Publishing Group, 4255 West Touhy Avenue,
Lincolnwood (Chicago), Illinois 60646-1975 U.S.A.
All rights reserved. No part of this book may be reproduced, stored
in a retrieval system, or transmitted in any form or by any means,
electronic, mechanical, photocopying, recording or otherwise, without
the prior permission of NTC Publishing Group.
Manufactured in Hong Kong.

TABLE OF CONTENTS

TRIP PREPARATION CHECKLIST

_____Obtain passport if traveling outside the U.S. (applications available at local post office). You will need:

    _____certified birth certificate (with raised seal), naturalization papers, or other proof of citizenship

    _____current photo ID or other descriptive ID

    _____two 2-inch-square recent photos

    _____application fee ($42, adults; $27, children up to age 17)

_____Obtain visas, if necessary, for any foreign countries you will be visiting.

_____Make transportation reservations:

    _____airline tickets

    _____rail passes

    _____car rental

    _____local public transit passes

_____Make lodging reservations.

_____Check on necessary immunizations, if any. Call The Centers for Disease Control, Division of Quarantine Foreign Travel, 404-639-2572.

_____If you'll be driving a car abroad, obtain an International Driving Permit from any AAA office.

_____Obtain traveler's checks.

_____Obtain small packets of local currency for each foreign country you'll be visiting to cover tips, taxi fare, or miscellaneous items until you are able to exchange money.

_____You may wish to arrange with your credit card company to participate in its electronic fund transfer service, if available, which will allow you to use your credit card to obtain cash from ATMs in U.S. and foreign cities.

For my part, I travel not to go anywhere, but to go. I travel for travel's sake. The great affair is to move.
Robert Louis Stevenson, *Travels with a Donkey*

_____You may with to obtain special travel health insurance, trip cancellation insurance, auto insurance, or life insurance.

_____Purchase a money belt and/or neck pouch for carrying passport, money, valuables, etc.

_____Leave your itinerary, a copy of your passport data page, airline ticket numbers, credit card numbers, and a list of your traveler's check numbers with a relative or friend. Make additional copies to keep with you in various places.

_____Prepare a list of names and addresses of friends and relatives to whom you'll want to write. (see pages 90–91)

_____Collect any guide books, maps, etc. that you'll wish to take along.

_____Obtain any prescription medicines you'll need to carry you through your trip, as well as a copy of eyeglass or contact lens prescriptions.

_____Stop your mail and newspapers. Or arrange for someone to pick these up, water your plants, and check on your house. Set light timers.

_____Several days before departure, reconfirm your flight reservations.

_____Make a list of the contents of each piece of luggage in case of loss. Keep this with you, not in your luggage.

_____Before you leave the house, check for:

_____wallet   _____hotel vouchers, etc.

_____tickets   _____transportation passes

_____cash   _____camera/film

_____traveler's checks   _____medication

_____necessary credit cards (leave all others home)

PACKING TIPS

- Travel light. Pack only what you absolutely need. If you'll be moving from place to place, no one will know your wardrobe is repetitive.

- Don't take anything you would hate to lose. Leave unnecessary credit cards, expensive jewelry, irreplaceable items, etc., at home.

- Avoid packing flashy clothes and jewelry. Don't draw attention to yourself as a wealthy tourist.

- If you can, pack everything in one carry-on bag. This will avoid the possibility of loss and waiting in long baggage claim lines.

- If you do check your baggage, at least pack a carry-on with essential toiletries, medication, spare glasses/contact lenses, and a clean shirt and underwear in the event your luggage is misdirected or lost.

- Consider transferring toiletries from large containers to smaller, plastic containers.

- When traveling abroad, keep all medicines in their original labeled containers. Pack a copy of all prescriptions and the generic name of each drug. If a medicine contains a narcotic, carry with you a letter of explanation from your physician.

- Lock your luggage and place a name and address label inside each piece. If you prefer, use a business address rather than your home address on the outer ID tag of your luggage.

- Mark your luggage with a distinctive identifier (colored tape or a bright ribbon tied to the handle or a Trav-A-Belt) so that it can be spotted quickly on the baggage conveyer with numerous look-alikes.

- Take along a lightweight, folding umbrella (keep this with you, not packed away) and/or a waterproof hooded jacket, as well as a middleweight neutral sweater, something that goes with everything.

- Pack an extra pair of shoes in case the first pair get soaked in a downpour. And never take brand new shoes. Break them in first.

- If you'll be doing a lot of walking, pack a lightweight backpack or carry-all to more easily carry guide books, snack food, purchases, sweater, umbrella, etc.

- When traveling abroad, if you must take electrical appliances, you'll need to take a converter (converts foreign electrical current to 110V) and adapter plugs (to adapt appliance plugs to foreign outlets). These come in a kit available at most luggage stores and travel centers.

- Miscellaneous items that could prove invaluable:

    _____pocket calculator

    _____pens/pencils, notepad

    _____paper clips, rubber bands, tape

    _____Swiss army knife

    _____small sewing kit, safety pins

    _____several small towels

    _____washcloths (these are almost nonexistent in Europe)

    _____travel alarm clock or alarm watch

    _____sunglasses, sunscreen/lotion

    _____a small container of laundry soap, a travel lingerie/ clothesline

    _____several zipper-type plastic bags of varying sizes (great for leaky bottles, wet things, etc.)

    _____an extra collapsible flight/sport bag in which to carry accumulated items on the return trip home

TRIP ITINERARIES

Departure: Date _____ Time _____

Destination: _____

Transportation/ _____
Route _____

_____

_____

Arrival: Date _____ Time _____

Accommodations _____

_____

Plans/Notes _____

_____

Departure: Date _____ Time _____

Destination: _____

Transportation/ _____
Route _____

_____

_____

Arrival: Date _____ Time _____

Accommodations _____

_____

Plans/Notes _____

_____

Traveling is no fool's errand to him who carried his eyes and itinerary along with him.
Amos Bronson Alcott, *Table Talk: Travel*

Departure:	Date	Time
Destination:		
Transportation/ Route		
Arrival:	Date	Time
Accommodations		
Plans/Notes		

Departure:	Date	Time
Destination:		
Transportation/ Route		
Arrival:	Date	Time
Accommodations		
Plans/Notes		

TRIP ITINERARIES

Departure: Date   Time
_____

Destination: _____

Transportation/
Route _____

_____

_____

Arrival: Date   Time
_____

Accommodations _____

_____

Plans/Notes _____

_____

Departure: Date   Time
_____

Destination: _____

Transportation/
Route _____

_____

_____

Arrival: Date   Time
_____

Accommodations _____

_____

Plans/Notes _____

_____

As a member of an escorted tour, you don't even have to know the Matterhorn isn't a tuba.

Temple Fielding

Departure:	Date	Time
Destination:		
Transportation/ Route		
Arrival:	Date	Time
Accommodations		
Plans/Notes		

Departure:	Date	Time
Destination:		
Transportation/ Route		
Arrival:	Date	Time
Accommodations		
Plans/Notes		

TRIP ITINERARIES

Departure:	Date	Time
Destination:		
Transportation/ Route		
Arrival:	Date	Time
Accommodations		
Plans/Notes		

Departure:	Date	Time
Destination:		
Transportation/ Route		
Arrival:	Date	Time
Accommodations		
Plans/Notes		

Methods of locomotion have improved greatly in recent years, but places to go remain about the same.
Don Herold

Departure:	Date	Time
Destination:		
Transportation/ Route		
Arrival:	Date	Time
Accommodations		
Plans/Notes		

Departure:	Date	Time
Destination:		
Transportation/ Route		
Arrival:	Date	Time
Accommodations		
Plans/Notes		

TRIP ITINERARIES

Departure: Date   Time

Destination:

Transportation/
Route

Arrival: Date   Time

Accommodations

Plans/Notes

Departure: Date   Time

Destination:

Transportation/
Route

Arrival: Date   Time

Accommodations

Plans/Notes

Travel, in the younger sort, is a part of education; in the elder, a part of experience. He that travelleth into a country before he hath some entrance into the language, goeth to school, and not to travel.

Francis Bacon, *Of Travel*

Departure:	Date	Time
Destination:		
Transportation/ Route		
Arrival:	Date	Time
Accommodations		
Plans/Notes		

Departure:	Date	Time
Destination:		
Transportation/ Route		
Arrival:	Date	Time
Accommodations		
Plans/Notes		

RECORD OF EXPENSES

Date	Item/ Service	Location	Method of Payment	Current Exch. Rate	Amount
				Total.....	

The heaviest baggage for a traveler is an empty purse.
German proverb

Date	Item/ Service	Location	Method of Payment	Current Exch. Rate	Amount
				Total.....	17

RECORD OF EXPENSES

Date	Item/Service	Location	Method of Payment	Current Exch. Rate	Amount

Total.....

The world is his who has money to go over it.
Emerson, *Conduct of Life: Wealth*

Date	Item/ Service	Location	Method of Payment	Current Exch. Rate	Amount
				Total	

RECORD OF EXPENSES

Date	Item/ Service	Location	Method of Payment	Current Exch. Rate	Amount
				Total	

Travel is hard on clothes, person, and purse.
Eleazar, *Midrash Tehillim*

Date	Item/ Service	Location	Method of Payment	Current Exch. Rate	Amount
				Total	

ACCOMMODATIONS NOTES

Lodging name

Location

Telephone

Dates stayed   Room number

Comments

Lodging name

Location

Telephone

Dates stayed   Room number

Comments

*In America there are two classes of travel—first class,
and with children.*
Robert Benchley, *Kiddie-Kar Travel*

Lodging name

Location

Telephone

Dates stayed   Room number

Comments

Lodging name

Location

Telephone

Dates stayed   Room number

Comments

ACCOMMODATIONS NOTES

Lodging name

Location

Telephone

Dates stayed   Room number

Comments

Lodging name

Location

Telephone

Dates stayed   Room number

Comments

My heart is warm with the friends I make,
And better friends I'll not be knowing;
Yet there isn't a train I wouldn't take,
No matter where it's going.

Edna St. Vincent Millay, *Travel*

Lodging name

Location

Telephone

Dates stayed   Room number

Comments

Lodging name

Location

Telephone

Dates stayed   Room number

Comments

ACCOMMODATIONS NOTES

Lodging name

Location

Telephone

Dates stayed   Room number

Comments

Lodging name

Location

Telephone

Dates stayed   Room number

Comments

The man who goes alone can start today; but he who
travels with another must wait till that other is ready.
Henry D. Thoreau, *Walden*, ch. 1

Lodging name

Location

Telephone

Dates stayed   Room number

Comments

Lodging name

Location

Telephone

Dates stayed   Room number

Comments

DINING NOTES

Restaurant name

Location

_____

Telephone

Date

Comments

_____

_____

_____

_____

Restaurant name

Location

_____

Telephone

Date

Comments

_____

_____

_____

_____

This summer one third of the nation will be ill-housed,
ill-nourished, and ill-clad. Only they call it a vacation.
Joseph Salak

Restaurant name

Location

Telephone

Date

Comments

Restaurant name

Location

Telephone

Date

Comments

DINING NOTES

Restaurant name

Location

Telephone

Date

Comments

Restaurant name

Location

Telephone

Date

Comments

Travel teaches toleration.
Disraeli, *Contarini Fleming*, 1932

Restaurant name

Location

Telephone

Date

Comments

Restaurant name

Location

Telephone

Date

Comments

DINING NOTES

Restaurant name

Location

Telephone

Date

Comments

Restaurant name

Location

Telephone

Date

Comments

*Not bound to swear allegiance to any master, wher-
ever the wind takes me I travel as a visitor.*

Horace

Restaurant name

Location

Telephone

Date

Comments

Restaurant name

Location

Telephone

Date

Comments

METRIC MEASURES AND U.S. EQUIVALENTS

Length and Distance _____

1 millimeter (mm)		= .0394 in.
1 centimeter (cm)	= 10mm	= .3937 in.
1 meter (m)	= 1000mm	= 1.0396 yd.
1 kilometer (km)	= 1000m	= .6214 mi.

Weight _____

1 milligram (mg)		= .0154 grain
1 gram (g)	= 1000 mg	= .0353 oz.
1 kilogram (kg)	= 1000 g	= 2.2046 lb.

Volume _____

1 milliliter (ml)		= .0610 cu. in.
1 centiliter (cl)	= 10 ml	= .6102 cu. in.
1 deciliter (dl)	= 10 cl	= 6.1025 cu. in.
1 liter (l)	= 10 dl	= 1.057 qt. or .2642 gal.

Area _____

1 sq. centimeter	= 100 sq. mm	= .155 sq. in.
1 sq. meter	= 10,000 sq. cm	= 1.196 sq. yd.
1 sq. kilometer		= .3861 sq. mi.

The swiftest traveller is he that goes afoot.
Henry D. Thoreau, *Walden*, ch. 1

Conversion Table

If you know:	Multiply by:	To find:
millimeters	.04	inches
centimeters	.4	inches
meters	1.1	yards
kilometers	.6	miles
grams	.035	ounces
kilograms	2.2	pounds
milliliters	.034	fl. ounces
liters	2.1	pints
liters	1.06	quarts
liters	.26	gallons
sq. centimeters	.16	sq. inches
sq. meters	1.2	sq. yards
sq. kilometers	.4	sq. miles
C°	1.8 (then add 32)	F°

Fahrenheit (°F.) temperatures

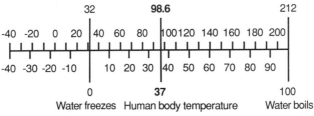

Celsius (°C) temperatures

U.S. MEASURES AND METRIC EQUIVALENTS

Length and Distance

1 inch (in.)		= 2.54 cm
1 foot (ft.)	= 12 in.	= 30.48 cm
1 yard (yd.)	= 3 ft.	= .9144 m
1 mile (mi.)	= 5,280 ft.	= 1.6093 km
1 nautical mile	= 1.151 mi.	= 1.852 km

Weight

1 grain (gr.)		= .0648 g
1 dram (dr.)	= 27.3438 gr.	= 1.7718 g
1 ounce (oz.)	= 16 dr.	= 28.35 g
1 pound (lb.)	= 16 oz.	= .4536 kg

Volume

1 fluid ounce (fl. oz.)		= 2.957 cl
1 pint (pt.)	= 16 fl. oz.	= .4732 l
1 quart (qt.)	= 2 pt.	= .946 l
1 gallon (gal.)	= 4 qt.	= 3.7853 l

Area

1 sq. inch		= 6.5416 sq. cm
1 sq. foot	= 144 sq. in.	= .093 sq. m
1 sq. yard	= 9 sq. ft.	= .8361 sq. m
1 sq. mile		= 2.59 sq. km

Traveling may be. . . an experience we shall always re-
member, or an experience which, alas, we shall never
forget.

J. Gordon, *Your Sense of Humor,* 1930

_____ Conversion Table _____

If you know:	Multiply by:	To find:
inches	25.0	millimeters
feet	30.0	centimeters
yards	.9	meters
miles	1.6	kilometers
ounces	28.0	grams
pounds	.45	kilograms
fl. ounces	30.0	milliliters
pints	.47	liters
quarts	.95	liters
gallons	3.8	liters
F°	.557 (after first subtracting 32)	C°

Travel, for those with their eyes and ears open, is a great university on the go. The classes and lectures are in the world's museums, galleries, cathedrals, and great buildings. They are also held in all the deep forests, alpine meadows, great deserts, and sweeping shorelines of this planet. Best of all, you are your own professor.

Lewis N. Clark

AVERAGE WORLD TEMPERATURES (F°)

| | January | | July | |
	High	Low	High	Low
Acapulco, Mexico	85	70	89	75
Amsterdam, The Netherlands	40	34	69	59
Athens, Greece	54	42	90	72
Atlanta, Georgia	53	36	89	70
Auckland, New Zealand	73	60	56	46
Bangkok, Thailand	89	67	90	76
Belgrade, Yugoslavia	37	27	84	61
Berlin, Germany	35	26	74	55
Bern, Switzerland	35	26	74	56
Bogota, Colombia	67	48	64	50
Boston, Mass.	40	20	84	60
Budapest, Hungary	35	26	82	61
Buenos Aires, Argentina	85	63	57	42
Cairo, Egypt	65	47	96	70
Calcutta, India	80	55	90	79
Calgary, Alberta, Canada	26	5	76	49
Cape Town, South Africa	78	60	63	45
Caracas, Venezuela	75	56	78	61
Casablanca, Morocco	63	44	79	64
Chicago, Ill.	33	17	75	64
Copenhagen, Denmark	36	29	72	55
Dallas, Tex.	55	36	95	76
Damascus, Syria	53	36	96	64
Denver, Colo.	42	16	87	58
Dublin, Ireland	47	35	67	51
Edinburgh, Scotland	43	35	65	52
Geneva, Switzerland	39	29	77	58
Hamilton, Bermuda	68	58	85	73
Helsinki, Finland	27	17	71	57
Hong Kong	64	56	87	78
Honolulu, Hawaii	77	67	82	74

	January		July	
	High	**Low**	**High**	**Low**
Houston, Tex.	61	50	88	76
Istanbul, Turkey	45	36	81	65
Jerusalem, Israel	55	41	87	63
Lagos, Nigeria	88	74	83	74
La Paz, Bolivia	63	43	62	33
Las Vegas, Nev.	55	33	105	76
Lima, Peru	82	66	67	57
Lisbon, Portugal	56	46	79	63
London, England	44	35	73	55
Los Angeles, Calif.	65	45	83	62
Madrid, Spain	47	33	87	62
Manila, Philippines	86	69	88	75
Mexico City, Mexico	66	42	74	54
Miami, Fla.	76	58	89	75
Minneapolis, Minn.	23	6	85	63
Montreal, Quebec, Canada	23	8	79	62
Moscow, Soviet Union	21	9	76	55
Nairobi, Kenya	77	54	69	51
Nassau, Bahamas	77	65	88	75
New Delhi, India	71	43	95	80
New Orleans, La.	64	48	90	76
New York, N.Y.	40	26	82	67
Oslo, Norway	30	20	73	56
Ottawa, Ontario, Canada	21	3	80	58
Paris, France	42	32	76	55
Philadelphia, Pa.	41	25	87	66
Phoenix, Ariz.	65	35	105	75
Portland, Ore.	44	35	79	58
Prague, Czechoslovakia	34	25	74	58
Quebec City, Quebec, Canada	18	2	76	57
Regina, Saskatchewan, Canada	12	-7	81	52

AVERAGE WORLD TEMPERATURES (F°)

	January High	January Low	July High	July Low
Rio de Janeiro, Brazil	84	73	75	63
Rome, Italy	54	39	88	64
St. Louis, Mo.	41	26	90	72
Salt Lake City, Utah	36	17	92	61
San Francisco, Calif.	56	40	69	52
San Juan, Puerto Rico	81	67	87	74
Santiago, Chile	85	53	59	37
Seattle, Wash.	43	31	75	53
Shanghai, China	47	32	91	75
Singapore	86	73	88	75
Stockholm, Sweden	31	23	70	55
Sydney, Australia	78	65	60	46
Tokyo, Japan	47	29	83	70
Toronto, Ontario, Canada	31	18	81	61
Vancouver, B.C., Canada	42	33	74	55
Vienna, Austria	34	26	75	59
Warsaw, Poland	30	21	75	56
Washington, D.C.	44	29	87	68
Wellington, New Zealand	69	56	53	42
Winnipeg, Manitoba, Canada	9	–8	80	57

Sources: *World Almanac*
Information Please Almanac

U.S. MILEAGE CHART

UNITED STATES MILEAGE CHART

Column key (abbreviations): ABQ = Albuquerque, N. Mex.; ATL = Atlanta, Ga.; BHM = Birmingham, Ala.; BOS = Boston, Mass.; CHI = Chicago, Ill.; CLE = Cleveland, Ohio; DAL = Dallas, Tex.; DEN = Denver, Colo.; DET = Detroit, Mich.; HOU = Houston, Tex.; IND = Indianapolis, Ind.; KC = Kansas City, Mo.; LA = Los Angeles, Calif.; MEX = Mexico City, Mex.; MIA = Miami, Fla.; MSP = Minneapolis, Minn.; MTL = Montreal, Que.; NAS = Nashville, Tenn.; NOL = New Orleans, La.; NYC = New York, N.Y.; OMA = Omaha, Nebr.; PHL = Philadelphia, Pa.; PHX = Phoenix, Ariz.; POR = Portland, Ore.; STL = St. Louis, Mo.; SLC = Salt Lake City, Utah; SFO = San Francisco, Calif.; SEA = Seattle, Wash.; TOR = Toronto, Ont.; DC = Washington, D.C.

From \ To	ABQ	ATL	BHM	BOS	CHI	CLE	DAL	DEN	DET	HOU	IND	KC	LA	MEX	MIA	MSP	MTL	NAS	NOL	NYC	OMA	PHL	PHX	POR	STL	SLC	SFO	SEA	TOR	DC
Albuquerque, N. Mex.	—	1381	1251	2172	1281	1560	638	417	1525	834	1266	782	807	1414	1938	1190	2087	1218	1134	1979	858	1899	432	1371	1038	604	1115	1440	1647	1824
Atlanta, Ga.	1381	—	150	1037	674	722	795	1398	724	789	493	798	2182	1768	665	1068	1190	242	479	841	986	741	1793	2601	541	1878	2496	2618	959	608
Birmingham, Ala.	1251	150	—	1165	657	736	645	1286	709	567	491	648	2054	1618	751	1006	1321	191	343	988	836	891	1665	2477	500	1750	2368	2490	1007	736
Boston, Mass.	2172	1037	1165	—	963	628	1748	1949	695	1804	906	1391	2979	2783	1504	1368	318	1088	1507	206	1412	296	2604	3046	1141	2343	3095	2976	539	429
Chicago, Ill.	1281	674	657	963	—	335	917	996	266	1067	181	499	2054	2045	1329	405	828	446	912	802	459	738	1713	2083	289	1390	2142	2013	492	671
Cleveland, Ohio	1560	722	736	628	335	—	1159	1321	170	1253	294	779	2367	2367	1253	740	561	530	1138	473	784	413	1992	2418	529	1715	2467	2348	287	346
Dallas, Tex.	638	795	645	1748	917	1159	—	781	1143	243	865	489	1387	1138	1300	936	1705	660	496	1552	644	1552	1009	2009	630	1242	1753	2078	1369	1319
Denver, Colo.	417	1398	1286	1949	996	1321	781	—	1253	1058	1058	600	1059	1746	2037	841	1815	1156	1273	1771	537	1691	792	1238	857	504	1235	1307	1479	1616
Detroit, Mich.	1525	724	709	695	266	170	1143	1253	—	1265	278	743	2311	2311	1352	671	528	562	1045	637	716	571	1957	2349	513	1647	2399	2279	226	506
Houston, Tex.	834	789	567	1804	1067	1253	243	1058	1265	—	987	743	1538	710	1187	1157	1827	711	356	1610	841	1508	1149	2205	779	1438	1912	2274	1491	1375
Indianapolis, Ind.	1266	493	491	906	181	294	865	1058	278	987	—	485	1965	1965	1148	587	713	278	840	713	633	643	1698	2227	235	1504	2256	2194	504	558
Kansas City, Mo.	782	798	648	1391	499	779	489	600	743	743	485	—	1627	1627	1589	447	1305	556	806	1198	201	1214	1214	1809	235	1115	1845	1757	715	1043
Los Angeles, Calif.	807	2182	2054	2979	2054	2367	1387	1059	2311	1538	1965	1627	—	1917	2687	1889	2873	2025	1883	2786	1595	2706	389	959	1845	715	379	1131	2537	2651
Mexico City, Mex.	1414	1768	1618	2783	2045	2367	1138	1746	2311	710	1965	1627	1917	—	2169	2074	2805	1747	1335	2805	1747	2487	1549	2785	1757	2016	2291	2852	2469	2354
Miami, Fla.	1938	665	751	1504	1329	1253	1300	2037	1352	1187	1148	1589	2687	2169	—	1723	1654	917	860	1308	1654	1198	2298	3256	1196	2532	3053	3221	1509	1075
Minneapolis, Minn.	1190	1068	1006	1368	405	740	936	841	671	1157	587	447	1889	2074	1723	—	1074	826	1163	1207	357	1207	1591	1678	552	1186	1940	1608	897	1076
Montreal, Que.	2087	1181	1270	318	828	561	1705	1815	528	1827	713	1305	2873	2805	1654	1074	—	1163	1654	378	1074	1591	2209	2961	1075	2209	2961	2751	336	579
Nashville, Tenn.	1218	242	191	1088	446	530	660	1156	562	711	278	556	2025	1747	917	826	1163	—	517	892	744	792	1650	2359	299	1494	2249	2376	754	659
New Orleans, La.	1134	479	343	1507	912	1138	496	1273	1045	356	840	806	1883	1335	860	1163	1654	517	—	1311	1311	1311	1738	2505	673	1738	2359	2815	1271	1078
New York, N.Y.	1979	841	988	206	802	473	1552	1771	637	1610	713	1198	2786	2805	1308	1207	378	892	1311	—	1251	100	2411	2885	948	2182	2934	2815	469	233
Omaha, Nebr.	858	986	836	1412	459	784	644	537	716	841	633	201	1595	1747	1654	357	1074	744	1311	1251	—	1251	1290	1638	449	931	1683	1638	942	1116
Philadelphia, Pa.	1899	741	891	296	738	413	1552	1691	571	1508	643	1214	2706	2487	1198	1207	1591	792	1311	100	1251	—	2331	2868	868	2114	2866	2751	453	133
Phoenix, Ariz.	432	1793	1665	2604	1713	1992	1009	792	1957	1149	1698	1214	389	1549	2298	1591	2209	1650	1738	2411	1290	2331	—	1266	1470	648	763	1437	2183	2566
Portland, Ore.	1371	2601	2477	3046	2083	2418	2009	1238	2349	2205	2227	1809	959	2785	3256	1678	2961	2359	2505	2885	1638	2868	1266	—	2060	767	636	648	175	2754
St. Louis, Mo.	1038	541	500	1141	289	529	630	857	513	779	235	257	1845	1757	1196	552	1075	299	673	948	449	868	1470	2060	—	1470	2089	2081	739	793
Salt Lake City, Utah	604	1878	1750	2343	1390	1715	1242	504	1647	1438	1504	1115	715	2016	2532	1186	2209	1494	1738	2182	931	2114	648	767	1337	—	752	836	808	2496
San Francisco, Calif.	1115	2496	2368	3095	2142	2467	1753	1235	2399	1912	2256	1845	379	2291	3053	1940	2961	2249	2359	2934	1683	2866	763	636	2089	752	—	808	2625	2799
Seattle, Wash.	1440	2618	2490	2976	2013	2348	2078	1307	2279	2274	2194	1757	1131	2852	3221	1608	2815	2376	2815	2815	1638	2751	1437	175	2081	836	808	—	2684	2799
Toronto, Ont.	1647	959	1007	539	492	287	1369	1479	226	1491	504	715	2537	2469	1509	897	336	754	1271	469	942	453	2566	2754	739	808	2625	2684	—	456
Washington, D.C.	1824	608	736	429	671	346	1319	1616	506	1375	558	1043	2651	2354	1075	1076	579	659	1078	233	1116	133	2566	2754	793	2047	2799	2684	456	—

©1987 by Rand McNally—TDM, Inc., R.L. 90-S-89

INTERNATIONAL CLOTHING SIZE COMPARISON CHART

Men

Suits, Pants, Overcoats, Sweaters

United States	34	35	36	37		38	39		40	41		42
Great Britain	34	35	36	37		38	39		40	41		42
Europe		44	46	48	49½	51	52½		54	55½		57

Socks

United States	9½		10		10½		11		11½
Great Britain	9½		10		10½		11		11½
Europe	38–39		39–40		40–41		41–42		42–43

Shoes

United States	7		8	9	10	11		12	13
Great Britain	6		7	8	9	10		11	12
Europe	39½		41	42	43	44½		46	47

Shirts

United States	14	14½	15	15½	15¾	16	16½	17	17½	18
Great Britain	14	14½	15	15½	15¾	16	16½	17	17½	18
Europe	36	37	38	39	40	41	42	43	44	45

Hats

United States	6¾	6⅞	7		7⅛	7¼	7⅜	7½	7⅝
Great Britain	6⅝	6¾	6⅞	7		7⅛	7¼	7⅜	7½
Europe	54	55	56	57	58	59	60	61	

Women

Blouses, Sweaters

United States	10	12	14	16	18	20	22	24
	(30)	(32)	(34)	(36)	(38)	(40)	(42)	(44)
Great Britain	32	34	36	38	40	42	44	46
Europe	38	40	42	44	46	48	50	52

> *Why seek Italy,*
> *Who cannot circumnavigate the sea*
> *Of thoughts and things at home?*
>
> Emerson, *The Day's Ration*

Dresses, Coats, Suits, Skirts, Pants

United States	8	10	12	14	16	18	20
Great Britain	30	32	33	35	36	38	39
Europe		36	38	40	42	44	46	48

Shoes

U.S.	4	4½	5	5½	6	6½	7	7½	8	8½	9	9½	10
G.B.	2½	3	3½	4	4½	5	5½	6	6½	7	7½	8	8½
Europe	35	35½	36	36½	37	37½	38	38½	39	39½	40	40½	41

Stockings

United States	8	8½	9	9½	10	10½	11
Great Britain	8	8½	9	9½	10	10½	11
Europe	0	1	2	3	4	5	6

Kids

Dresses, Coats, Suits, Skirts, Pants—Junior Misses

United States	2	4	6	8	10	13	15
Great Britain	2	4	6	8	10	13	15
Europe	1	2	5	7	9	10	12

Shoes—Girls and Boys

United States	8	9	10	11	12	13	1	2	3	4½
Great Britain	7	8	9	10	11	12	13	1	2	3
Europe	24	25	27	28	29	30	32	33	34	36

Most Apparel—Girls and Boys

United States	3	4	5	6	6X
Great Britain	18	20	22	24	26
Europe	98	104	110	116	122

U.S. EMBASSY TELEPHONE NUMBERS WORLDWIDE

When available, country codes (in brackets) and city codes (in parentheses) are given, which you may or may not need to use depending on whether you are dialing from within the country and/or city.

Country	City	Embassy Telephone Number
Algeria	Algiers	[213] (2) 601-425; 601-255; 601-186
Argentina	Buenos Aires	[54] (1) 774-7611; 774-8811; 774-9911
Australia	Canberra	[61] (62) 705000
Austria	Vienna	[43] (222) 31-55-11
Bahamas	Nassau	(809) 322-1181; 328-2206
Barbados	Bridgetown	(809) 436-4950
Belgium	Brussels	[32] (2) 513-3830
Belize	Belize City	[501] (2) 77161
Benin	Cotonou	[229] 30-06-50
Boliva	La Paz	[591] (2) 350251; 350120
Brazil	Brasilia	[55] (6) 321-7272
Bulgaria	Sofia	[359] (2) 88-48-01 to 05
Burundi	Bujumbura	[257] (2) 23454
Cameroon	Yaounde	[237] 234014
Canada	Ottawa, Ontario	(613) 238-5335
Central African Republic	Bangui	61-02-00
Chad	N'Djamena	[235] (51) 62-18; 40-09
Chile	Santiago	[56] (2) 710133; 710190; 710326; 710375
China	Beijing	[86] (1) 532-3831
Colombia	Bogota	[57] (1) 285-1300; 285-1688
Congo	Brazzaville	83-20-70; 83-26-24
Costa Rica	San Jose	[506] 20-39-39
Cuba (Swiss Embassy)	Havana	320551; 320543
Czechoslovakia	Prague	[42] (2) 53 6641; 53 6649

The shortest distance between two points is under construction.

Noelie Alito

Country	City	Embassy Telephone Number
Denmark	Copenhagen	[45] (31) 42-31-44
Djibouti	Djibouti	[253] 35-39-95
Dominican Republic	Santo Domingo	(809) 541-2171
Ecuador	Quito	[593] (2) 562-890
Egypt	Cairo	[20] (2) 355-7371
El Salvador	San Salvador	[503] 26-7100
Equatorial Guinea	Malabo	2406; 2507
Ethiopia	Addis Ababa	[251] (01) 551002
Fiji	Suva	[679] 314-466
Finland	Helsinki	[358] (0) 171931
France	Paris	[33] (1) 42-96-12-02; 42-61-80-75
Gambia	Banjul	[220] 92856; 92858
Germany, East	Berlin	[37] (2) 2202741
Germany, West	Bonn	[49] (228) 3391
Ghana	Accra	775347; 775297; 775298
Greece	Athens	[30] (1) 721-2951; 721-8401
Grenada	St. George's	(809) 440-1731; 440-1734
Guatemala	Guatemala City	[502] (2) 31-15-41
Haiti	Port-Au-Prince	[509] (1) 20354; 20368; 20200; 20612
Honduras	Tegucigalpa	[504] 32-3120
Hungary	Budapest	[36] (1) 112-6450
Iceland	Reykjavik	[354] (1) 29100
India	New Delhi	[91] (11) 600651
Indonesia	Jakarta	[62] (21) 360-360
Iraq	Baghdad	[964] (1) 719-6138; 719-6139; 718-1840; 719-3791
Ireland	Dublin	[353] (1) 687122
Israel	Tel Aviv	[972] (3) 654338

U.S. EMBASSY TELEPHONE NUMBERS WORLDWIDE

Country	City	Embassy Telephone Number
Italy	Rome	[39] (6) 46741
Ivory Coast	Abidjan	[225] 21-09-79; 21-46-72
Jamaica	Kingston	(809) 929-4850
Japan	Tokyo	[81] (3) 224-5000
Jordan	Amman	[962] (6) 644-371
Kenya	Nairobi	[254] (2) 334141
Korea	Seoul	[82] (2) 732-2601 to 18
Kuwait	Kuwait	[965] 242-4151 to 59
Laos	Vientiane	2220; 2357; 2384; or 3570 and 2357 after office hours
Lebanon	Beirut	[961] 417774; 415802; 415803; 402200; 403300
Luxembourg	Luxembourg	[352] 460123
Malaysia	Kuala Lumpur	[6] (03) 248-9011
Malta	Valletta	[356] 623653; 620424
Mexico	Mexico City	[52] (5) 211-0042
Morocco	Rabat	[212] (7) 622-65
The Netherlands	The Hague	[31] (70) 62-49-11
New Zealand	Wellington	[64] (4) 722-068
Nicaragua	Managua	[505] (2) 666010; 666013; 666015 to 18; 666026 to 27; 666032 to 34
Nigeria	Lagos	[234] (1) 610097
Norway	Oslo	[47] (2) 44-85-50
Pakistan	Islamabad	[92] (51) 826161 to 79
Panama	Panama City	[507] 27-1777
Peru	Lima	[51] (14) 338-000
Philippines	Manila	[63] (2) 521-7116
Poland	Warsaw	[48] (22) 283041 to 49
Portugal	Lisbon	[351] (1) 726-6600; 726-6659; 726-8670; 726-8880

As the Spanish proverb says, "He who would bring home the wealth of the Indies must carry the wealth of the Indies with him." So it is in traveling: a man must carry knowledge with him, if he would bring knowledge home.

Samuel Johnson

Country	City	Embassy Telephone Number
Romania	Bucharest	[40] (0) 10-40-40
Saudi Arabi	Riyadh	[966] (1) 488-3800
Senegal	Dakar	[221] 23-59-28; 23-11-85
Seychelles	Victoria	23921; 23922
Sierra Leone	Freetown	26481
South Africa	Pretoria	[27] (12) 28-4266
Soviet Union	Moscow	252-2451 to 59
Spain	Madrid	[34] (1) 276-3400; 276-3600
Sudan	Khartoum	74700; 74611
Sweden	Stockholm	[46] (8) 783-5300
Switzerland	Bern	[41] (31) 437-011
Syria	Damascus	[963] (11) 333052; 332557; 330416; 332814; 332315
Thailand	Bangkok	[66] (2) 252-5040
Trinidad & Tobago	Port-of-Spain	(809) 622-6372; 622-6376; 622-6176
Turkey	Ankara	[90] (4) 126 54 70
Uganda	Kampala	[256] (41) 259791 to 93; 259795
United Kingdom	London	[44] (01) 499-9000
Venezuela	Caracas	[58] (2) 285-3111; 285-2222
Yugoslavia	Belgrade	[38] (11) 645-655
Zaire	Kinshasa	[243] (12) 25881 to 86
Zambia	Lusaka	[260] (1) 228-595; 228-596; 228-598
Zimbabwe	Harare	[263] (4) 794-521

MAJOR HOLIDAYS

Albania: Jan 1 & 2, January 11 (Republic Proclamation Day), May 1, Nov 28 (Independence Day), Nov 29 (Liberation Day)

Argentina: Jan 1, Maundy Thursday (optional), Good Friday, May 1 (Labor Day), May 25 (Anniversary of the 1810 Revolution), June 10 (Malvinas Day), June 20 (Flag Day), July 9 (Independence Day), Aug 17 (Anniversary of San Martin's Death), Oct 12 (Columbus Day), Dec 8 (Immaculate Conception), Dec 25

Australia: Jan 1, Jan 26 (Australia Day), Good Friday, Easter, Easter Monday, Apr 25 (Veterans' Day), Queen's Birthday (second Monday in June), Dec 25 & 26

Austria: Jan 1, Jan 6, Easter Monday, May 1, Ascension Day (five weeks after Easter), Whit Monday (eight weeks after Easter), Aug 15, Oct 26 (National Day), Nov 1, Dec 8 (Immaculate Conception Day), Dec 25 & 26 (On Saturdays, many shops are open only until noon.)

Barbados: Jan 1, Good Friday, Easter Mon, May 1 (May Day), Whit Monday, Kadoment Day (varies), United Nations Day (first Mon in Oct), Nov 30 (Independence Day), Dec 25 & 26

Belgium: Jan 1, Easter Monday, Ascension Day, Whit Monday, May 1, July 21 (National Day), Aug 15, Nov 1, Nov 11 (Armistice Day), Nov 15 (Dynasty Day), Dec 25, Dec 26 (informally)

Botswana: Jan 1 & 2, Good Friday, Easter Sat, Easter Mon, Ascension Day, July 19 (President's Day), Sept 30 (Botswana Day), Oct 1 (Public Holiday), Dec 25-27

Brazil: Jan 1, Carnival (4 days before Ash Wed), Good Friday, Easter, Apr 21 (Tiradentes Day), May 1 (Labor Day), Corpus Christi, Sept 7 (Independence Day), Oct 12 (Feast of Brazil's patron saint), Nov 2 (All Souls' Day), Nov 15 (Proclamation of the Republic), Dec 25, Dec 31

Bulgaria: Jan 1, Mar 8 (Women's Day), May 1 & 2 (Labor Day), May 24 (Culture Day), Sept 9 & 10 (National Day), Nov 7 (Soviet Revolution Day)

Canada: Jan 1, Good Friday, Easter Monday, Monday before May 25 (Queen's birthday), July 1 (Dominion Day), first Monday in Sept (Labour Day), second Monday in Oct (Thanksgiving Day), Nov 11 (Rememberance Day), Dec 25

Chile: Jan 1, Holy Week, May 1, May 21, Aug 15, Sept 11, Sept 18-19, Oct 12, Nov 1, Dec 8, Dec 25

China: Jan 1, Spring Festival/Chinese New Year (late Jan/early Feb), Mar 8 (Internat'l Women's Day), May 1 (Internat'l Labour Day), May 4 (Chinese Youth Day), July 1 (Communist Day), Aug 8 (People's Liberation Army Day), Oct 1 (National Day)

Congo: Jan 1, May 1 (Labour Day), July 31 (Readjustment of Revolution), Aug 13–15 (Les Trois Glorieuses), All Saints Day, Dec 25, Dec 31

Cyprus: Jan 1, Jan 6 (Ephiphany Day), Mar 25 (Greek Independence Day), Greek Orthodox Good Friday, Greek Orthodox Easter Sat, Greek Orthodox Easter Mon, May 1 (Labour Day), Oct 28 (Greek Oxi Day), Dec 25 & 26

Czechoslovakia: Jan 1, Easter Monday, May 1, May 9 (National Day), Dec 25 & 26

Denmark: Jan 1, Maundy Thursday, Good Friday, Monday after Easter, Two weeks after Easter (Common Prayers Day), May 1 (p.m. only), Ascension Day, Whit Monday, June 5 (Constitution Day), Dec. 24-26

Egypt: First day of Ramadan (early spring, varies with sightings of the moon), June 18 (Evacuation Day), Eid al-Fitr (late spring, varies with sightings of the moon), July 23 (Revolution Day), Eid al-Adha (midsummer, varies with sightings of the moon), Hijra

MAJOR HOLIDAYS

(midsummer, varies with sightings of the moon), Al-Ashoura (midsummer, varies with sightings of the moon), Prophet's Birthday (midautumn, varies with sightings of the moon), Oct 6 (Victory Day)

Finland: Jan 1, Jan 10 (Epiphany), Good Friday, Easter Monday, May 1, Ascension Day, Whit Saturday, Midsummer Eve and Midsummer Day, Oct 31 (All Saints' Day), Dec 6 (Independence Day), Dec 24-26

France: Jan 1, Easter Monday, May 1, May 8, July 14 (Bastille Day), Aug 15, Nov 1, Nov 11 (Armistice Day), Dec 25 (August is a holiday month. Many businesses are closed. Gov't offices are minimally staffed.)

Germany, East: Jan 1, Good Friday, Whit Monday, May 1, Oct 7 (German Democratic Republic Day), Dec 25 & 26

Germany, West: Jan 1, Good Friday, Easter Monday, May 1, Ascension Day, Whit Monday, June 17 (German Unity Day), Nov 1 (in Catholic areas only), Prayer Day (mid-Nov), Dec 25 & 26

Great Britain: Jan 1, Jan 2 (Scotland only), Mar 1 (St. David's Day—Wales only), Good Friday, Easter Monday, first Monday in May (May Day), last Monday in May (Spring Bank Holiday), first Monday (Scotland only) or last Monday (rest of G.B.) in August (Summer Bank Holiday), Dec 25 & 26

Greece: Jan 1, Jan 6, Shrove Monday (Monday before Lent), Mar 25 (Independence Day), May 1, Good Friday, Easter Monday, Aug 15, Oct 28 (National Day), Dec 25 & 26

Hungary: Jan 1, Apr 4 (Liberation Day), Easter Monday, Aug 20 (Constitution Day), Nov 7 (Soviet Revolution Day), Dec 25 & 26

India: Jan 1, Jan 26 (Republic Day), Holi (during Mar), Ram Navami (during Mar), Good Friday, Id-Ul-Fir (during May), Aug 15 (Independence Day), Muharram (during Aug), Janamashtmi (during Sept/Oct), Dussehra (during Oct), Oct 2 (Ghandi's birthday), Diwali (during Oct/Nov), Dec 25

Ireland: Jan 1, Mar 17 (St. Patrick's Day), Good Friday, Easter Monday, first Monday in June (June Bank Holiday), first Monday in Aug (Aug Bank Holiday), Oct 31 (Halloween), Dec 25 & 26

Israel: Each Sabbath (sundown Friday to sunset Saturday), Passover (early Apr), May 6 (Holocaust Day), May 13 (Memorial Day), May 14 (Independence Day), Shavuot (seven weeks after Passover), Rosh Hashana (2 days in Sept), Yom Kippur (10 days after Rosh Hashana), Sukkoth (5 days after Yom Kippur)

Italy: Jan 1, Easter Monday, Apr 25 (Liberation Day), May 1, Aug 15, Nov 1, Dec 8 (Immaculate Conception Day), Dec 25 & 26

Japan: Jan 1-3, Jan 15 (Adults' Day), Feb 11 (National Foundation Day), Már 20 or 21 (Vernal Equinox Day), Apr 29 (Emperor's Birthday), May 3 (Constitution Memorial Day), May 5 (Children's Day), Sept 15 (Respect for the Aged Day), Sept 23 or 24 (Autumnal Equinox Day), Oct 10 (Health Sports Day), Nov 3 (Culture Day), Nov 23 (Labour Thanksgiving Day)

Kenya: Jan 1, Good Friday, Easter Mon, Ramadan (late Apr), May 1 (Labour Day), Eid el-Fitr (late spring, varies with sightings of the moon), June 1 (Madaraka), Oct 20 (Kenyatta Day), Dec 12 (Republic Day), Dec 25 & 26

Korea, South: Jan 1-3, Folklore Day (during Jan/Feb), Mar 1 (Independence Movement Day), Apr 5 (Arbor Day), May 5 (Children's Day), Buddha's Birthday (during May), June 6 (Memorial Day), July 17 (Constitution Day), Aug 15 (Liberation Day), Oct 1 (Armed Forces Day), Oct 3 (National Foundation Day), Ch'usok or Thanksgiving (during Sept/Oct), Oct 9 (Korean Alphabet Day), Dec 25

Luxembourg: Jan 1, Shrove Tuesday, Easter Monday, Ascension Day, Whit Monday, May 1, June 23 (Grand Duke's Birthday), Nov 1 & 2, Dec 25 & 26

Malawi: Jan 1, Mar 3 (Martyr's Day), Good Friday, Easter Sat, Easter Mon, May 14 (Kamuzu Day), July 6 (Republic Day), Aug 3

MAJOR HOLIDAYS

(Aug Holiday), Oct 17 (Mothers Day), Dec 25 & 26

Mexico: Jan 1, Feb 5 (Constitution Day), Mar 21 (Benito Juarez's Birthday), May 1 (Labor Day), May 5 (Anniversary of the Battle of Puebla), Sept 1 (President's Message to Congress), Sept 6 (Independence Day), Oct 12 (Columbus Day), Nov 20 (Mexican Revolution Anniversary), Dec 11-12 (Feast Day of Mexico's patron saint), Dec 25

Mozambique: Jan 1, Feb 3 (Heroes' Day), Apr 7 (Mozambican Women's Day), May 1 (Labour Day), June 25 (Independence & Foundation of Frelimo Day), Sept 7 (Victory Day), Sept 25 (Armed Forces Day), Dec 25

Netherlands: Jan 1, Good Friday (though many shops remain open at least part of the day), Easter Monday, Apr 30 (Queen's Day), Ascension Day, Whit Monday, Dec 5 (St. Nicholas' Day), Dec. 25 & 26

Norway: Jan 1, Maundy Thursday, Good Friday, Easter Monday, May 1, May 17 (Independence Day), Ascension Day, Whit Monday, Dec 24 (p.m. only), Dec 25 & 26, Dec 31 (p.m. only)

Philippines: Jan 1, Easter, Apr 19 (Bataan Day), May 1 (Labour Day), June 12 (Independence Day), July 4 (Philippine-American Friendship Day), All Saints Day, Nov 30 (National Heroes' Day), Dec 25, Dec 30 (Rizal Day)

Poland: Jan 1, Easter Monday, May 1, May 9 (Victory Day), Corpus Christi (date varies), July 22 (National Day), Nov 1, Dec 25 & 26

Portugal: Jan 1, Shrove Tuesday, Good Friday, Apr 25 (Liberty Day), May 1, June 10 (National Day), June 13 (St. Anthony's Day —Lisbon only), June 24 (St. John's Day—Oporto only), Aug 15, Oct 5 (Proclamation of the Republic), Nov 1, Dec 1 (Independence Day), Dec 8 (Immaculate Conception Day), Dec 24 & 25

Romania: Jan 1 & 2, May 1 & 2, Aug 23 & 24 (National Days), Dec 25 (informally—most shops remain open)

I always love to begin a journey on Sundays, because I shall have the prayers of the church, to preserve all that travel by land, or by water.

Jonathan Swift

South Africa: Jan 1, Good Friday, Easter Mon, Ascension Day, May 31 (Republic Day), Sept 7 (Settlers' Day), Oct 10 (Kruger Day), Dec 16 (Day of the Covenant), Dec 17 (Public Holiday), Dec 25 & 26

Soviet Union: Jan 1 & 2, May 1 & 2, May 9 (Victory Day), Nov 7 & 8 (Days of the Revolution), Dec 5 (Constitution Day)

Spain: Jan 1, Jan 6, Mar 19 (St. Joseph's Day), Maundy Thursday, Good Friday, May 1, Corpus Christi (date varies), July 25 (St. James' Day), Aug 15, Oct 12 (Columbus Day), Dec 8 (Immaculate Conception Day), Dec 25 (Each city holds a festival for its patron saint once a year during which all work halts for several days.)

Sweden: Jan 1, Jan 6, Good Friday, Easter Monday, May 1, May 28 (Ascension Day), Whit Monday, Midsummer Day (June, near the solstice), Oct 31 (All Saints' Day), Dec 25 & 26

Switzerland: Jan 1 & 2, Good Friday, Easter Monday, Ascension Day, Whit Monday, Aug 1 (Independence Day), Dec 25 & 26

Tanzania: Jan 12 (Zanzibar Revolution Day), Feb 5 (CCM Day), Good Friday, Easter Mon, Apr 26 (Union Day), May 1 (May Day), Eid el-Fitr (late spring, varies with sightings of the moon), July 7 (Peasants Day), Eid el-Haj (midsummer, varies with sightings of the moon), Maulid (midautumn, varies with sightings of the moon), Dec 9 (Independence Day), Dec 25

Turkey: Apr 23 (National Day), May 1, May 19 (Youth Day), May 27 & 28 (Constitution Days), Aug 30 (Victory Day), Oct 29 & 30 (Declaration of the Republic Days)

Venezuela: Jan 1, Carnival Mon & Tues, Apr 19 (Proclamation of Independence), Easter Thursday, Good Friday, May 1 (Labor Day), June 24 (Battle of Carabobo), July 5 (Independence Day), July 24 (Bolivar's Birthday), Oct 12 (Columbus Day), Dec 24 & 25

Yugoslavia: Jan 1 & 2, May 1 & 2, July 4 (Partisan Day), Nov 29 & 30 (Republic Days)

U.S. STATE TOURISM OFFICES

Telephone numbers are subject to change.

ALABAMA
Bureau of Tourism & Travel
532 S. Perry St.
Montgomery, AL 36104
205-261-4169 or
  1-800-ALABAMA (out of
  state) 1-800-392-8096 (in
  state)

ALASKA
Alaska Division of Tourism
P.O. Box E
Juneau, AK 99811
907-465-2010

ARIZONA
Arizona Office of Tourism
1100 West Washington
Phoenix, AZ 85007
602-255-3618

ARKANSAS
Arkansas Department of
  Parks and Tourism
1 Capitol Mall
Little Rock, AR 72201
501-682-7777 or 1-800-482-8999
  or 1-800-643-8383 (out of
  state)

CALIFORNIA
California Office of Tourism
Department of Commerce
1121 L Street
Suite 103
Sacramento, CA 95814
916-322-2881

COLORADO
Colorado Tourism Board
1625 Broadway, Suite 1700
Denver, CO 80202
303-592-5410

CONNECTICUT
Tourism Promotion Service
Connecticut Department of
  Economic Development
210 Washington St.
Hartford, CT 06106
203-566-3948 or 1-800-842-7492
  (in state) 1-800-243-1685
  (Maine through Virginia)

DELAWARE
Delaware Tourism Office
Delaware Development
  Office
99 Kings Highway
P.O. Box 1401
Dover, DE 19903
302-736-4271 or 1-800-441-8846

DISTRICT OF COLUMBIA
Washington Convention and
  Visitors Association
Suite 250
1575 Eye Street, NW
Washington, D.C. 20005
202-789-7000

FLORIDA
Department of Commerce
   Visitors Inquiry
126 Van Buren St.
Tallahassee, FL 32399-2000
904-487-1462

GEORGIA
Tourist Division
P.O. Box 1776
Atlanta, GA 30301
404-656-3590 or
   1-800-VISIT-GA

HAWAII
Hawaii Visitors Bureau
2270 Kalakaua Ave., Suite 801
Honolulu, HI 96815
808-923-1811

IDAHO
Department of Commerce
700 W. State St. Second Floor
Boise, ID 83720
208-334-2470 or 1-800-635-7820

ILLINOIS
Illinois Department of
   Commerce and
   Community Affairs, Office
   of Tourism
620 East Adams Street
Springfield, IL 62701
217-782-7139

INDIANA
Indiana Dept. of Commerce
Tourism Division
1 North Capitol, Suite 700
Indianapolis, IN 46204
317-232-8860

IOWA
Iowa Department of
   Economic Development
Bureau of Tourism and
   Visitors
200 East Grand Avenue
Des Moines, IA 50309
515-281-3100

KANSAS
Travel & Tourism
   Development Division
Department of Commerce
400 W. 8th St., 5th Floor
Topeka, KS 66603
913-296-2009

KENTUCKY
Department of Travel
   Development
Capital Plaza Tower
Frankfort, KY 40601
502-564-4930 or 1-800-225-TRIP
(Continental United States
   and provinces of Ontario
   and Quebec, Canada)

U.S. STATE TOURISM OFFICES

LOUISIANA
Office of Tourism
P.O. Box 94291
Baton Rouge, LA 70804-9291
504-342-8119 or
    1-800-33GUMBO

MAINE
Maine Publicity Bureau
97 Winthrop St., P.O. Box
    2300
Hallowell, ME 04347-2300
207-289-2423

MARYLAND
Office of Tourist
    Development
217 E. Redwood St.
Baltimore, MD 21202
301-974-3517

MASSACHUSETTS
Dept. of Food & Agriculture
Bureau of Markets
100 Cambridge St.
Boston, MA 02202
617-272-3018

MICHIGAN
Travel Bureau
Department of Commerce
P.O. Box 30226
Lansing, MI 48909
1-800-5432-YES

MINNESOTA
Minnesota Office of Tourism

375 Jackson St.
250 Skyway Level
Farm Credit Services Bldg.
St. Paul, MN 55101
612-296-5029 or 1-800-328-1461
    (out of state) 1-800-652-9747
    (in state)

MISSISSIPPI
Division of Tourism
Department of Economic
    Development
P.O. Box 849
Jackson, MS 39205
601-359-3414 or 1-800-647-2290

MISSOURI
Missouri Division of Tourism
Truman State Office Bldg.
301 W. High St.
P.O. Box 1055
Jefferson City, MO 65102
314-751-4133

MONTANA
Travel Montana
Department of Commerce
1424 9th Ave.
Helena, MT 59620
406-444-2654 or 1-800-541-1447

NEBRASKA
Dept. of Economic
    Development
Division of Travel and
    Tourism

> *It is not worth while to go round the world to count the*
> *cats in Zanzibar.*
>
> Henry D. Thoreau, *Walden*, conclusion

301 Centennial Mall South
P.O. Box 94666
Lincoln, NE 68509
402-471-3796 or 1-800-742-7595
   or 1-800-228-4307 (out of
   state)

NEVADA
Commission on Tourism
Capitol Complex
Carson City, NV 89710
1-800-Nevada-8

NEW HAMPSHIRE
Office of Vacation Travel
P.O. Box 856
Concord, NH 03301
603-271-2666

NEW JERSEY
Division of Travel and
   Tourism
CN-826
Trenton, NJ 08625
609-292-2470

NEW MEXICO
New Mexico Tourism &
   Travel Division ED & TD
Room 119, Joseph M.
   Montoya Bldg.
1100 St. Francis Dr.
Santa Fe, NM 87503
505-827-0291 or 1-800-545-2040

NEW YORK
Division of Tourism
1 Commerce Plaza
Albany, NY 12245
518-474-4116 or 1-800-225-5697
   (Cont. U.S., Puerto Rico,
   Virgin Is.)

NORTH CAROLINA
Travel and Tourism Division
Department of Commerce
430 North Salisbury St.
Raleigh, NC 27611
919-733-4171 or 1-800-VISIT NC

NORTH DAKOTA
North Dakota Tourism
   Promotion
Liberty Memorial Building
Capitol Grounds
Bismarck, ND 58505
701-224-2525 or 1-800-437-2077
   (out of state)

OHIO
Ohio Division of Travel and
   Tourism
P.O. Box 1001
Columbus, OH 43266–0101
614-466-8844 (Business Office)
   1-800-BUCKEYE (National
   Toll-Free Travel Hotline)

OKLAHOMA
Oklahoma Tourism and
   Recreation Dept.

U.S. STATE TOURISM OFFICES

Literature Distribution
  Center
215 NE 28th Street
Oklahoma City, OK 73105
405-521-2409 (in Oklahoma &
  states not mentioned
  below)
  1-800-652-6552 (in AR, CO,
  KS, MO, NM, and TX
  except area code 512)

OREGON
Tourism Division
Oregon Economic
  Development
595 Cottage St., NE
Salem, OR 97310
503-378-3451 or 1-800-547-7842
  (out of state)

PENNSYLVANIA
Bureau of Travel
  Development
453 Forum Building
Harrisburg, PA 17120
717-787-5453 (Business Office)
  1-800-VISIT PA, ext. 275
  (Consumer Information)

RHODE ISLAND
Rhode Island Tourism
  Division
7 Jackson Walkway
Providence, RI 02903
401-277-2601 or 1-800-556-2484
  (For residents from Maine
  to Virginia/West Virginia
  and Northern Ohio)

SOUTH CAROLINA
South Carolina Division of
  Tourism
Box 71
Columbia, SC 29202
803-734-0122

SOUTH DAKOTA
Department of Tourism
Capitol Lake Plaza
Pierre, South Dakota 57501
605-773-3301 or 1-800-843-1930
  (out of SD) 1-800-952-2217
  (in SD)

TENNESSEE
Department of Tourist
  Development
P.O. Box 23170
Nashville, TN 37202
615-741-2158

TEXAS
Travel Information Services
State Highway Department
P.O. Box 5064
Austin, TX 78763-5064
512-463-8971

UTAH
Utah Travel Council
Council Hall, Capitol Hill
Salt Lake City, UT 84114
801-538-1030

VERMONT
Agency of Development and
  Community Affairs

Only fools want to travel all the time; sensible men want to arrive.

Klemens von Metternich

Travel Division
134 State St.
Montpelier, VT 05602
802-828-3236

VIRGINIA
Virginia Division of Tourism
202 North Ninth Street
Suite 500
Richmond, VA 23219
804-786-4484

WASHINGTON
Washington State Dept. of
  Trade and Economic
  Development
101 General Administration
  Bldg.
  AX-13
Olympia, WA 98504
206-753-5630

WASHINGTON, D.C.
See District of Columbia

WEST VIRGINIA
Dept. of Commerce
State Capitol Complex
Charleston, WV 25305
304-348-2286 or
  1-800-CALL-WVA

WISCONSIN
Department of Development
Division of Tourism
  Development

Box 7606
Madison, WI 53707
608-266-2161 or
  1-800-ESCAPES (in WI and
  neighbor states)

WYOMING
Wyoming Travel Commission
I-25 at College Drive
Cheyenne, WY 82002-0660
307-777-7777 or 1-800-225-5996

AMERICAN SAMOA
Off. of Development
  Planning
Pago Pago, AS 96799
684-633-5155

**NORTHERN MARIANA
  ISLANDS**
Marianas Visitors Bur.
Off. of the Governor
Saipan, CM 96950
670-234-8327

PUERTO RICO
Tourism Co.
P.O. Box 4435
San Juan, PR 00903
809-721-2400

VIRGIN ISLANDS
Dept. of Human Services
Barbel Plaza S.
St. Thomas, VI 00802
809-774-0930

Source: *Information Please Almanac*

TIPS FOR CAR TRAVEL

- Be sure your car is properly tuned and checked before embarking on your trip.

- Equip your car with a pair of jump cables, a first-aid kit, a blanket, and necessary, up-to-date maps.

- Prepare your car for the climate in which you'll be driving. Be sure coolant/antifreeze levels are appropriate.

- If you'll be driving through desert areas, carry extra water for drinking as well as for the car radiator, and plenty of canned fruit juice and snacks in case of an emergency. Stop often to let your engine and tires cool off.

- Familiarize yourself with the traffic laws of the city/state/country in which you'll be driving.

- Check gas costs. Know what to expect.

- Although your U.S. drivers license will usually suffice in most countries abroad, some do require an International Driving Permit. The five-language format will facilitate explanations in most countries should you be stopped by local officers. Obtain one from any AAA Motor Club office.

- Stay away from large cities unless you're comfortable driving in traffic congestion. Perhaps park on the outskirts of a metropolitan area and use public transportation. Or sightsee in cities on weekends and drive into the country during the week.

- If traveling in countries where left-hand side of the road driving is required, try to get acclamated in less congested areas.

- If traveling with children, take along a variety of things to keep them occupied, such as paper and pencil, crayons, activity books, a deck of cards, a cassette player and tapes, travel games, and books or magazines.

Thanks to the Interstate Highway System, it is now possible to travel from coast to coast without seeing anything.

Charles Kuralt

- Pack some cassette tapes for everyone to enjoy. Perhaps coordinate your music selections with the area of the country in which you'll be traveling. (e.g., *The Grand Canyon Suite* by Grofe if you're touring the Grand Canyon)

- Always buckle up!

When renting a car:
- Make your reservations before you leave home so that you can choose your options and likely get a reduced rate.

- If a car model is unfamiliar to you, inquire about seating capacity, space, etc. Be sure the car is right for your needs.

- If traveling in West Germany, keep in mind that driving on the *autobahns* where there is no speed limit requires a car with adequate "pick-up." Merging and changing lanes can be frightening. Try to rent a car with adequate engine power.

- Inquire about insurance, which should be included with the rental. Collision damage waiver (CDW), or additional coverage that may be purchased to avoid paying damage costs, is generally optional. Most auto insurance policies cover cars rented in the United States but not those rented abroad. Some credit card companies will cover all damages if you charge the car rental, in which case you can decline the expensive CDW.

- If traveling abroad, consider packing some cassette tapes of your choosing. (More than likely your rental car will come equipped with a cassette player.) Unless you're fluent in the language, you may have difficulty listening to foreign radio. Again, perhaps you'd like to coordinate your tape selections with the area of your travels. (e.g., *Siegfried's Rhine Journey* by Wagner if you'll be driving along the Rhine River).

TIPS FOR AIR TRAVEL

- Purchase your ticket well in advance to save money.

- When you pick up your ticket, check to see that all information is correct, your name is spelled correctly, and that you have a coupon for each flight.

- Write down the ticket number and date and place of purchase. Keep this in your wallet or another safe place.

- Treat airline tickets like cash. If you do loose your ticket, immediately call the airline's refund department. Have the ticket number, date and place of purchase ready.

- Special dietary requirements should be made at least 24 hours before departure but preferably should be made at the time of your reservation.

- Confirm your flight departure before leaving for the airport.

- Take all unnecessary tags off your luggage. All you need on the outside of your bag is an ID and the flight tag for where it's going *this* trip.

- When flying across several time zones, to avoid "jet lag":

    - Begin your tip well rested; go to bed early for several nights before flying to prepare for the time change.

    - Drink a glass of water hourly while airborne and no alcoholic beverages.

    - If possible, plan your arrival late in the day and go right to bed. If you must fly at night, try to sleep for most of the trip.

    - Write for a free copy of Argonne National Laboratory's anti-jet lag diet and follow it for three days prior to departure. Send a stamped, self-addressed envelope to: Argonne Nat'l Laboratory, 9700 South Cass Ave., Argonne, IL 60439.

*If you don't miss a few planes during the year you are
spending too much time at airports.*

Paul C. Martin

- If you often experience painful ear blockages while flying, taking an antihistamine just before takeoff and landing may help.

- If traveling with infants, bring along an infant seat restraint. Don't hold your child on your lap.

- Bring games, toys, and books to occupy children.

- If traveling with children, request bulkhead seating. These are the seats just behind the compartment wall with no seats in front and more foot room and space for children and their paraphenalia.

- If your luggage is misdirected to another city and you need underwear and a shirt for an important meeting tomorrow, although they don't advertise it, most airlines will accommodate you provided your demands aren't excessive. Ask. You may get help.

When I was very young and the urge to be someplace else was on me, I was assured by mature people that maturity would cure this itch. When years described me as mature, the remedy prescribed was middle age. In middle age I was assured that greater age would calm my fever, and now that I am fifty-eight perhaps senility will do the job.

John Steinbeck, *Travels with Charley*

TIPS FOR OCEAN/CRUISE TRAVEL

- Book your cruise early (6 months) to get the best choices of date, accommodations, and itinerary as well as a substantial discount.

- Study the various cruise lines before you make a choice. Evaluate and consider such items as cost, size (ratio of passengers to public rooms), personality (fun, family, upscale), style (casual, informal, formal), and length of cruise.

- Some lines offer special rates for a third or fourth person sharing a room with two full-fare passengers. This savings can be divided equally to realize a substantial savings for all travelers. And children are often discounted when sharing a room with parents.

- Cancellations are often frequent. If your first choice is booked, get on a waiting list.

- Check on who your passenger-mates will be. Unlike hotels, once checked in you can't check out. During school holidays, cruise ships are often filled with college students and children. If that poses a problem for you, book at another time.

- Outside cabins (with a porthole) will allow you to check the weather at a glance.

- If you suffer from motion sickness, talk to your physician about effective cures. Take any medication well before the ship sets sail. (With modern stabilizers on most ships, this generally isn't a problem.)

- If you have special dietary needs, tell your travel agent or the line itself well ahead of sailing. They'll be happy to accommodate you.

Never a ship sails out of the bay
But carries my heart as a stowaway.
Roselle Mercier Montgomery, *The Stowaway*

- Storage/closet space is minimal on newer cruise ships so try to keep your wardrobe small and/or coordinated. Use the mix and match method.

- Travel irons are frowned on or often forbidden on some ships. Pack permanent press items.

- Pack enough clothes, however, to last the trip. Some lines have laundry service at a charge, but there is not enough room to wash even small items and hang them around your cabin to dry.

- Although the bulk of your cruise is paid for ahead of time, take some cash for bar charges, gift shop purchases, special services, and shore excursions. Check ahead to see if the ship accepts credit cards. You'll need traveler's checks or cash to exchange money at the ship's bank to use in foreign ports.

- Shore excursions are optional and cost extra. You may prefer to share a taxi.

- For cruises that go to foreign countries, proof of citizenship is needed. A passport is recommended, although a certified birth certificate, military discharge papers, U.S. notarized affidavit of citizenship, or a voter registration card will suffice.

- At cruise end, on the night before arrival in your home port, your luggage will be picked up in the wee hours. Be sure to leave out the clothes and toiletries you will need to get off the ship in the morning.

- For tipping suggestions on cruises, see Tipping Guidelines on pages 74–75.

TIPS FOR RAIL TRAVEL

- Consider and evaluate various classes of rail travel depending on whether you can sleep sitting up; will accept a footrest, pillow, and blanket; or require a bed.

- Don't burden yourself with excess or heavy baggage. You'll have to haul it yourself and swing it up and down from overhead racks.

- Arrive well before scheduled train departure. At stations where a train begins its journey, you can usually board a half hour before departure and thus get "settled in."

- If you plan to do a lot of traveling by rail in Europe, purchase a Eurailpass. It's an all-inclusive ticket good on railroads, certain buses, ferries, steamers, and hydrofoils in Europe. It must be purchased from an authorized U.S. agent before you leave for Europe. A Britrail pass will allow you similar rights in Great Britain. It also must be purchased before you leave the States.

- Consider traveling at night. This leaves daytime for sightseeing and saves money on hotel accommodations.

- Some European trains do not serve food. Check first and either eat before boarding or pack a lunch.

- Your ticket entitles you only to the space specified on it. Don't fill up adjoining seats with extra baggage.

- Take along books, magazines, or other means of diversion should you get bored with the scenery.

- If traveling with children, bring along plenty of things to keep them occupied—activity books, travel games, paper, pencil, crayons, cassette player and tapes (with headphones so as not to disturb other travelers).

- Some trains stock a limited supply of baby food. It would be wise, however, to bring your own if traveling with infants.

WORLD MONETARY UNITS

Afghanistan	Afghani
Albania	Lek
Algeria	Dinar
Andorra	French franc and Spanish peseta
Angola	Kwanza
Antigua and Barbuda	East Caribbean dollar
Argentina	Austral
Australia	Australian dollar
Austria	Schilling
Bahamas	Bahamian dollar
Bahrain	Bahrain dinar
Bangladesh	Taka
Barbados	Barbados dollar
Belgium	Belgian franc
Belize	Belize dollar
Benin	Franc CFA
Bhutan	Ngultrum
Bolivia	Peso boliviano
Botswana	Pula
Brazil	Cruzado
Brunei	Brunei dollar
Bulgaria	Lev
Burkina Faso	Franc CFA
Burma	Kyat
Burundi	Burundi franc
Cambodia	Riel
Cameroon	Franc CFA
Canada	Canadian dollar
Cape Verde	Cape Verde escudo
Central African Republic	Franc CFA
Chad	Franc CFA
Chile	Peso
China (Peoples Repub. of China)	Yuan
(Taiwan—Republic of China)	New Taiwan dollar
Colombia	Peso
Comoros	Franc CFA

WORLD MONETARY UNITS

Congo	Franc CFA
Costa Rica	Colón
Cuba	Peso
Cyprus	Cyprus pound
Czechoslovakia	Koruna
Denmark	Krone
Djibouti	Djibouti franc
Dominica	East Caribbean dollar
Dominican Republic	Peso
Ecuador	Sucre
Egypt	Egyptian pound
El Salvador	Colón
Equatorial Guinea	CFA franc
Ethiopia	Birr
Fiji	Fijian dollar
Finland	Markka
France	Franc
Gabon	Franc CFA
Gambia	Dalasi
Germany, East	Mark of the Deutsche Demokratische
Germany, West	Deutsche Mark
Ghana	Cedi
Greece	Drachma
Grenada	East Caribbean dollar
Guatemala	Quetzal
Guinea	Guinean franc
Guinea-Bissau	Guinea-Bissau peso
Guyana	Guyana dollar
Haiti	Gourde
Honduras	Lempira
Hungary	Forint
Iceland	New krona
India	Rupee
Indonesia	Rupiah
Iran	Rial
Iraq	Iraqi dinar

People travel for the same reason as they collect works of art: because the best people do it.

Aldous Huxley

Ireland	Irish pound (punt)
Israel	Shekel
Italy	Lira
Ivory Coast	Franc CFA
Jamaica	Jamaican dollar
Japan	Yen
Jordan	Jordanian dinar
Kenya	Kenyan shilling
Kiribati	Australian dollar
Korea, North	Won
Korea, South	Won
Kuwait	Kuwaiti dinar
Laos	Kip
Lebanon	Lebanese pound
Lesotho	Loti
Liberia	Liberian dollar
Libya	Libyan dinar
Liechtenstein	Swiss franc
Luxembourg	Luxembourg franc
Madagascar	Malagasy franc
Malawi	Kwacha
Malaysia	Ringgit
Maldives	Maldivian rupee
Mali	Franc CFA
Malta	Maltese lira
Mauritania	Ouguyia
Mauritius	Mauritian rupee
Mexico	Peso
Monaco	French franc
Mongolia	Tugrik
Morocco	Dirham
Mozambique	Metical
Nauru	Australian dollar
Nepal	Nepalese rupee
The Netherlands	Guilder
New Zealand	New Zealand dollar

WORLD MONETARY UNITS

Nicaragua	Cordoba
Niger	Franc CFA
Nigeria	Naira
Norway	Krone
Oman	Omani rial
Pakistan	Pakistan rupee
Panama	Balboa
Papua New Guinea	Kina
Paraguay	Guarani
Peru	Inti
The Philippines	Peso
Poland	Zloty
Portugal	Escudo
Qatar	Qatari riyal
Romania	Leu
St. Kitts and Nevis	East Caribbean dollar
St. Lucia	East Caribbean dollar
St. Vincent and the Grenadines	East Caribbean dollar
San Marino	Italian lira
São Tomé and Príncipe	Dobra
Saudi Arabia	Riyal
Senegal	Franc CFA
Seychelles	Seychelles rupee
Sierra Leone	Leone
Singapore	Singapore dollar
Solomon Islands	Solomon Islands dollar
Somalia	Somali shilling
South Africa	Rand
Soviet Union	Ruble
Spain	Peseta
Sri Lanka	Sri Lanka rupee
Sudan	Sudanese pound
Suriname	Suriname guilder

Down to Gehenna or up to the Throne,
He travels the fastest who travels alone.
Rudyard Kipling, *The Winners*

Swaziland	Lilangeni
Sweden	Krona
Switzerland	Swiss franc
Syria	Syrian pound
Tanzania	Tanzanian shilling
Thailand	Baht
Togo	Franc CFA
Tonga	Pa'anga
Trinidad and Tobago	Trinidad and Tobago dollar
Tunisia	Tunisian dinar
Turkey	Turkish lira
Tuvalu	Australian dollar
Uganda	Ugandan shilling
United Arab Emirates	Dirham
United Kingdom	Pound sterling
United States	Dollar
Uruguay	Peso
Vanuatu	Vatu
Vatican City State	Lira
Venezuela	Bolivar
Vietnam	Dong
Western Samoa	Tala
Yemen	Yemen dinar
Yemen Arab Republic	Rial
Yugoslavia	Dinar
Zaire	Zaire
Zambia	Kwacha
Zimbabwe	Zimbabwean dollar

Source: *Information Please Almanac*

TIPPING GUIDELINES

In general, reward those who have treated you well.

In the United States:

- Waiters/waitresses—15%–20%

- Maitre d's, captains—only for special attentiveness

- Wine steward—10% of the wine bill

- Bellhops/porters—$1 per bag

- Doorman—$.50–$1 for hailing a taxi, $1 for carrying bags in

- Chambermaid—$1 per day per room (place in envelope marked "Chambermaid")

- Room service—15%

- Concierge—$2–$10 per each service performed (restaurant reservation, tour booking)

- Parking attendant—$1–$2

- Taxi drivers—18%–20% on fares up to $5, 15% on fares over $5

- Skycap—$1 per bag

Tipping in foreign countries can be cause for consternation. Check travel guides for specific countries or talk to the tourist bureau to be sure of local customs. Airline personnel are also a good source for current information. In many countries a service charge is added to the hotel or restaurant bill. Check if it's there before leaving a tip.

In Europe:

- Read the menu. If you see something like *service compris* or *servizio compresso* written somewhere on the menu, the tip is included in the prices listed and the waiter should not add any extra charges. Leave small change. If you see *service non compris*, *service en sus*, or *service net*, service is not included.

The traveled mind is the catholic mind educated from exclusiveness and egotism.
Amos Bronson Alcott, *Table Talk: Travel*

Watch for it on the bill. If not there, leave 15%. If you're not sure, ask.

- Tip maitre d', doorman, porter, chambermaid, or concierge for unusual or exceptional service.

- Tipping is an insult in Iceland.

- In Scandinavia, tipping is not common except in cases of exceptional service.

- Tip cab drivers 10%–15% if a service charge has not been included in the meter fare. This is often the case in Belgium, Denmark, and the Netherlands. Ask.

- Tip washroom attendants and theater ushers if you use their services—as little as possible.

- In England, services are often hidden—listed on the menu but not on the bill. If service has been exceptional, add 5%. Never tip in bars or pubs.

- In Eastern European countries tips are frowned upon (if anyone is watching; otherwise they're accepted).

In Asia:

- This is generally a tip-free society. In many countries tipping is not only not expected, it's often considered an insult.

- In China, tour guides have begun to pass a hat. And employees of large hotels and restaurants frequented by Western tourists are better acquainted with the custom of tipping.

- In Japan there is *no tipping anywhere.* Although some hotels and restaurants may add a 10% service charge, there is no tipping beyond that. If you do give monetary reward for exceptional service, it must be wrapped in a piece of paper.

TIPPING GUIDELINES

In the South Pacific:

- Many islands forbid tipping.

- New Zealand is tip free.

- Tips are accepted, though not expected in Australia.

In South America:

- Tipping is generally optional and rendered with good service, though tips are usually appreciated.

- A service charge is often included in hotel and restaurant bills. If service has been particularly good, however, leave a small tip.

- Taxi drivers usually accept tips, although in some countries, such as Chile where tipping is not the custom, your tip might be returned.

In Mexico, Latin America, and Egypt:

- Tipping is expected for even the smallest service.

- Tip waiters even on top of the service charge added to your bill.

Tipping on Cruises:

- Tipping is done at journey's end, on the last full day of the cruise. Give your tips, in an envelope, directly to those you want to thank.

- Cabin steward—$2.50–$3 per passenger per day

- Dining room waiter—$2.50–$3 per passenger per day

- Busboy—$1–$2 per passenger per day

- Give slightly more to all of the above if you are traveling in a first class cabin on a first class luxury liner.

See one promontory, one mountain, one sea, one river, and see all.

Socrates

- Bartenders and deck stewards—10%–15% upon paying the bill

- Wine stewards—10%–15% upon paying the wine bill

- Room service (if not your regular cabin steward)—$1–$2 per call

Tipping Table:

Bill/Fare	15% Tip	Bill/Fare	15% Tip
$1	15¢	$26	$3.90
$2	30¢	$27	$4.05
$3	45¢	$28	$4.20
$4	60¢	$29	$4.35
$5	75¢	$30	$4.50
$6	90¢	$31	$4.65
$7	$1.05	$32	$4.80
$8	$1.20	$33	$4.95
$9	$1.35	$34	$5.10
$10	$1.50	$35	$5.25
$11	$1.65	$36	$5.40
$12	$1.80	$37	$5.55
$13	$1.95	$38	$5.70
$14	$2.10	$39	$5.85
$15	$2.25	$40	$6.00
$16	$2.40	$41	$6.15
$17	$2.55	$42	$6.30
$18	$2.70	$43	$6.45
$19	$2.85	$44	$6.60
$20	$3.00	$45	$6.75
$21	$3.15	$46	$6.90
$22	$3.30	$47	$7.05
$23	$3.45	$48	$7.20
$24	$3.60	$49	$7.35
$25	$3.75	$50	$7.50

MEDICAL TIPS FOR TRAVELERS

- If you have allergies, chronic ailments such as diabetes or asthma, or other unique medical problems, wear a medical alert bracelet or carry proper warnings on treatment in case of an emergency. Take with you all the drugs you'll need for the trip.

- The sun is dangerous at high altitudes. Be careful in the mountains. Use proper sun screen.

- Drink plenty of water when you're out in the sun.

- The sun is extremely intense in southern regions between 11 a.m. and 3 p.m. Consider lunch or indoor activities at those times.

- Consider carrying iodine pills as an emergency disinfectant in back-country areas where clean water may be a problem.

- Make sure all immunizations are up to date for the travel you'll be doing.

- When traveling abroad, if carrying medication containing a narcotic, consult the country's embassy for exact information before leaving to ensure you do not violate its laws. Occasionally what is not considered a narcotic in the U.S. may be illegal in other countries.

- If you are injured or become seriously ill while abroad, contact the nearest U.S. embassy. They will have a list of qualified English-speaking doctors and will help you obtain medical assistance. They will inform your family/friends at your request. But they *will not* pay for care.

- You can obtain a directory of certified English-speaking doctors and other health care providers by becoming a member of the International Association of Medical Assistance to Travelers (IAMAT). Membership is free but donations are appreciated. You will receive a membership card that entitles you to set fees for services. Contact: IAMAT, 417 Center St., Lewiston, NY 14092; 716-754-4883.

If you travel you see people in variety. But if you stay home you see them in development.

Upton Close

- Check with your insurance company about your medical coverage abroad. Obtain claim forms and take them with you. You will likely have to pay for services and be reimbursed upon return. Try to have the forms filled out in English. Note: Medicare benefits are not available in Europe.

- Consider obtaining emergency medical insurance before you travel abroad. The U.S. government will not pay for medical evacuation out of foreign countries.

- If you need a pharmacy at night while abroad, go to the nearest pharmacy. If it's closed, on the door will usually be the address of a pharmacy open that night.

- Most problems with water occur in Italy, Portugal, Spain, Latin and South America. To prevent diarrhea:

  - Avoid tap water that hasn't been purified, even for brushing teeth. Be wary of ice cubes.

  - Drink only tea, beer, wine, distilled liquor, bottle soft drinks, and carbonated water (opened at your table). Noncarbonated bottled water may or may not be safe.

  - Avoid local milk and milk products unless you're sure they've been pasteurized.

  - Avoid foods sold by street vendors, raw meat and fish, and salads. Stick to fruits and vegetables that you can peel yourself.

- To treat diarrhea:

  - Pepto-Bismol may prevent as well as cure diarrhea.

  - Many travelers take Lomotil to relieve diarrhea. However, it will lock in the infection, but you may have no choice if you're traveling.

  - Do not buy drugs for diarrhea abroad. Never buy Entero-vioform. It is banned in the U.S. and is said to cause serious complications.

CALORIE COUNTER

	Amount	Calories
Dairy products		
Cheese, cheddar	1 oz.	115
" , cottage	1 cup	220
" , cream	1 oz.	100
" , Swiss	1 oz.	105
" , American	1 oz.	82
Half-&-half	1 tbsp.	20
Milk, whole	1 cup	150
" , skim	1 cup	85
Milkshake, Chocolate	10.6 oz.	355
Ice cream	1 cup	270
Sherbet	1 cup	270
Yogurt, fruit-flavored	8 oz.	230
Eggs		
Fried, in butter	1	85
Hard-cooked	1	80
Scrambled, in butter, w/milk	1	95
Fats and oils		
Butter	1 tbsp.	100
Margarine	1 tbsp.	100
Salad dressing, blue cheese	1 tbsp.	75
" , French	1 tbsp.	65
" , Italian	1 tbsp.	85
Mayonnaise	1 tbsp.	100
Fruits and vegetables		
Apple, raw	1	80
Banana, raw	1	100

> *A good traveler is one who does not know where he is going to, and a perfect traveler does not know here he came from.*
>
> Lin Yutang

	Amount	Calories
Beans, green	1 cup	35
Broccoli, cooked	1 stalk	45
Cabbage, raw	1 cup	15
Cantaloupe	½	80
Carrot, raw	1	30
Celery, raw	1 stalk	5
Cherries, raw	10	45
Corn, cooked	1 ear	70
Corn, creamed	1 cup	210
Cucumber	6–8 slices	5
Fruit cocktail, canned, w/syrup	1 cup	195
Grapefruit, raw	½	45
Grapes	10	35
Lemonade	1 cup	105
Lettuce	1 cup	5
Mushrooms, raw	1 cup	20
Onions, raw	1 cup	65
Orange	1	65
Orange juice	1 cup	120
Peach, raw	1	40
Peaches, canned, w/syrup	1 cup	200
Pear, raw	1	100
Peas, cooked	1 cup	110
Potato, baked	1	145
Potato, French fried	10	110
Potato, mashed, w/milk	1 cup	135
Potato chips	10	115
Potato salad	1 cup	250
Raisins	1 cup	420
Spinach, cooked	1 cup	45
Strawberries, whole	1 cup	55
Tomato, raw	1	25
Tomato juice	1 cup	45

CALORIE COUNTER

	Amount	Calories
Grains		
Bagel, egg	1	165
Bread, white	1 slice	70
" , whole wheat	1 slice	65
Oatmeal	1 cup	130
Bran flakes	1 cup	105
Brownie, w/nuts	1	85
Corn flakes	1 cup	95
Cake, angel food	1/12 of cake	135
Cake, pound	1/17 of cake	160
Coffeecake	1/6 of cake	230
Cookies, chocolate chip	4	205
Cracker, saltines	4	50
Macaroni and cheese	1 cup	430
Noodles, cooked	1 cup	200
Pancake, plain	1	60
Pie, apple	1/7 of pie	345
Pizza, cheese, 12 in.	1/8	145
Popcorn, plain	1 cup	25
Rice, cooked	1 cup	180
Rolls	1	85
Spaghetti, w/meatballs and tomato sauce	1 cup	336
Meat, Poultry, Fish		
Bluefish, baked, w/butter	3 oz.	135
Crabmeat, canned	1 cup	135
Salmon, canned	3 oz.	120
Shrimp, French fried	3 oz.	190
Tuna, in oil	3 oz.	170

Travel is no longer any charm for me. I have seen all the foreign countries I want to see except heaven and hell, and I have only a vague curiosity as concerns one of those.

Mark Twain

	Amount	Calories
Bacon	2 slices	85
Ground beef, broiled	3 oz.	185
Roast beef, lean	3 oz.	165
Beef steak	3 oz.	330
Beef and vegetable stew	1 cup	220
Liver, beef	3 oz.	195
Ham	3 oz.	245
Pork chop	2.7 oz.	305
Frankfurter, cooked	1	170
Chicken, broiled	6.2 oz.	240
Chicken à la king	1 cup	470

Sugars and sweets

	Amount	Calories
Candy, milk chocolate	1 oz.	145
Candy, hard	1 oz.	110
Honey	1 tbsp.	65
Jams and preserves	1 tbsp.	55
Sugar, granulated	1 tbsp.	45

Miscellaneous

	Amount	Calories
Beer	12 fl. oz.	150
Gin, rum, vodka, whiskey (86 proof)	1.5 fl. oz.	105
Wine	3.5 fl. oz.	85
Cola	12 fl. oz.	145
Gelatin dessert	1 cup	140
Olives, green	4	15
Pickles, dill	1	5
Popsicle	1	70
Soup, cream of chicken, w/milk	1 cup	180
Soup, tomato, w/water	1 cup	90

Source: *World Almanac & Book of Facts*

DAILY RECORD OF TRAVELS

Day/date:

Place:

Weather:

Day's events/Thoughts/Ideas:

_____

_____

_____

_____

_____

_____

_____

Day/date:

Place:

Weather:

Day's events/Thoughts/Ideas:

_____

_____

_____

_____

_____

_____

_____

Long voyages, great lies
Italian proverb

Day/date: _____

Place: _____

Weather: _____

Day's events/Thoughts/Ideas: _____

_____

_____

_____

_____

_____

_____

_____

Day/date: _____

Place: _____

Weather: _____

Day's events/Thoughts/Ideas: _____

_____

_____

_____

_____

_____

_____

_____

DAILY RECORD OF TRAVELS

Day/date:

Place:

Weather:

Day's events/Thoughts/Ideas:

_____

_____

_____

_____

_____

_____

_____

Day/date:

Place:

Weather:

Day's events/Thoughts/Ideas:

_____

_____

_____

_____

_____

_____

_____

*Surely to have seen Athens gives a man what Swift
calls Invisible Precedence over his fellows.*
Sir Edward Marsh

Day/date:

Place:

Weather:

Day's events/Thoughts/Ideas:

Day/date:

Place:

Weather:

Day's events/Thoughts/Ideas:

DAILY RECORD OF TRAVELS

Day/date:

Place:

Weather:

Day's events/Thoughts/Ideas:

_____

_____

_____

_____

_____

_____

_____

_____

Day/date:

Place:

Weather:

Day's events/Thoughts/Ideas:

_____

_____

_____

_____

_____

_____

_____

_____

How much a dunce that has been sent to roam
Excels a dunce that has been kept at home!
William Cowper

Day/date:

Place:

Weather:

Day's events/Thoughts/Ideas:

_____

_____

_____

_____

_____

_____

_____

_____

Day/date:

Place:

Weather:

Day's events/Thoughts/Ideas:

_____

_____

_____

_____

_____

_____

_____

_____

DAILY RECORD OF TRAVELS

Day/date:

Place:

Weather:

Day's events/Thoughts/Ideas:

_____

_____

_____

_____

_____

_____

_____

Day/date:

Place:

Weather:

Day's events/Thoughts/Ideas:

_____

_____

_____

_____

_____

_____

_____

_____

I never travel without my diary. One should always have something sensational to read.

Oscar Wilde

Day/date: _____

Place: _____

Weather: _____

Day's events/Thoughts/Ideas: _____

_____

_____

_____

_____

_____

_____

_____

Day/date: _____

Place: _____

Weather: _____

Day's events/Ihoughts/Ideas: _____

_____

_____

_____

_____

_____

_____

_____

PHONE NUMBERS AND ADDRESSES

Name and address	Telephone
	( )
	( )
	( )
	( )
	( )
	( )
	( )
	( )

Name and address	Telephone
	( )
	( )
	( )
	( )
	( )
	( )
	( )
	( )

CALENDAR

1990

JANUARY

S	M	T	W	T	F	S
	1	2	3	4	5	6
7	8	9	10	11	12	13
14	15	16	17	18	19	20
21	22	23	24	25	26	27
28	29	30	31			

JULY

S	M	T	W	T	F	S
1	2	3	4	5	6	7
8	9	10	11	12	13	14
15	16	17	18	19	20	21
22	23	24	25	26	27	28
29	30	31				

FEBRUARY

S	M	T	W	T	F	S
				1	2	3
4	5	6	7	8	9	10
11	12	13	14	15	16	17
18	19	20	21	22	23	24
25	26	27	28			

AUGUST

S	M	T	W	T	F	S
			1	2	3	4
5	6	7	8	9	10	11
12	13	14	15	16	17	18
19	20	21	22	23	24	25
26	27	28	29	30	31	

MARCH

S	M	T	W	T	F	S
				1	2	3
4	5	6	7	8	9	10
11	12	13	14	15	16	17
18	19	20	21	22	23	24
25	26	27	28	29	30	31

SEPTEMBER

S	M	T	W	T	F	S
						1
2	3	4	5	6	7	8
9	10	11	12	13	14	15
16	17	18	19	20	21	22
23	24	25	26	27	28	29
30						

APRIL

S	M	T	W	T	F	S
1	2	3	4	5	6	7
8	9	10	11	12	13	14
15	16	17	18	19	20	21
22	23	24	25	26	27	28
29	30					

OCTOBER

S	M	T	W	T	F	S
	1	2	3	4	5	6
7	8	9	10	11	12	13
14	15	16	17	18	19	20
21	22	23	24	25	26	27
28	29	30	31			

MAY

S	M	T	W	T	F	S
		1	2	3	4	5
6	7	8	9	10	11	12
13	14	15	16	17	18	19
20	21	22	23	24	25	26
27	28	29	30	31		

NOVEMBER

S	M	T	W	T	F	S
				1	2	3
4	5	6	7	8	9	10
11	12	13	14	15	16	17
18	19	20	21	22	23	24
25	26	27	28	29	30	

JUNE

S	M	T	W	T	F	S
					1	2
3	4	5	6	7	8	9
10	11	12	13	14	15	16
17	18	19	20	21	22	23
24	25	26	27	28	29	30

DECEMBER

S	M	T	W	T	F	S
						1
2	3	4	5	6	7	8
9	10	11	12	13	14	15
16	17	18	19	20	21	22
23	24	25	26	27	28	29
30	31					

CALENDAR

1991

JANUARY
S	M	T	W	T	F	S
		1	2	3	4	5
6	7	8	9	10	11	12
13	14	15	16	17	18	19
20	21	22	23	24	25	26
27	28	29	30	31		

JULY
S	M	T	W	T	F	S
	1	2	3	4	5	6
7	8	9	10	11	12	13
14	15	16	17	18	19	20
21	22	23	24	25	26	27
28	29	30	31			

FEBRUARY
S	M	T	W	T	F	S
					1	2
3	4	5	6	7	8	9
10	11	12	13	14	15	16
17	18	19	20	21	22	23
24	25	26	27	28		

AUGUST
S	M	T	W	T	F	S
				1	2	3
4	5	6	7	8	9	10
11	12	13	14	15	16	17
18	19	20	21	22	23	24
25	26	27	28	29	30	31

MARCH
S	M	T	W	T	F	S
					1	2
3	4	5	6	7	8	9
10	11	12	13	14	15	16
17	18	19	20	21	22	23
24	25	26	27	28	29	30
31						

SEPTEMBER
S	M	T	W	T	F	S
1	2	3	4	5	6	7
8	9	10	11	12	13	14
15	16	17	18	19	20	21
22	23	24	25	26	27	28
29	30					

APRIL
S	M	T	W	T	F	S
	1	2	3	4	5	6
7	8	9	10	11	12	13
14	15	16	17	18	19	20
21	22	23	24	25	26	27
28	29	30				

OCTOBER
S	M	T	W	T	F	S
		1	2	3	4	5
6	7	8	9	10	11	12
13	14	15	16	17	18	19
20	21	22	23	24	25	26
27	28	29	30	31		

MAY
S	M	T	W	T	F	S
			1	2	3	4
5	6	7	8	9	10	11
12	13	14	15	16	17	18
19	20	21	22	23	24	25
26	27	28	29	30	31	

NOVEMBER
S	M	T	W	T	F	S
					1	2
3	4	5	6	7	8	9
10	11	12	13	14	15	16
17	18	19	20	21	22	23
24	25	26	27	28	29	30

JUNE
S	M	T	W	T	F	S
						1
2	3	4	5	6	7	8
9	10	11	12	13	14	15
16	17	18	19	20	21	22
23	24	25	26	27	28	29
30						

DECEMBER
S	M	T	W	T	F	S
1	2	3	4	5	6	7
8	9	10	11	12	13	14
15	16	17	18	19	20	21
22	23	24	25	26	27	28
29	30	31				

CALENDAR

1992

JANUARY

S	M	T	W	T	F	S
			1	2	3	4
5	6	7	8	9	10	11
12	13	14	15	16	17	18
19	20	21	22	23	24	25
26	27	28	29	30	31	

JULY

S	M	T	W	T	F	S
			1	2	3	4
5	6	7	8	9	10	11
12	13	14	15	16	17	18
19	20	21	22	23	24	25
26	27	28	29	30	31	

FEBRUARY

S	M	T	W	T	F	S
						1
2	3	4	5	6	7	8
9	10	11	12	13	14	15
16	17	18	19	20	21	22
23	24	25	26	27	28	29

AUGUST

S	M	T	W	T	F	S
						1
2	3	4	5	6	7	8
9	10	11	12	13	14	15
16	17	18	19	20	21	22
23	24	25	26	27	28	29
30	31					

MARCH

S	M	T	W	T	F	S
1	2	3	4	5	6	7
8	9	10	11	12	13	14
15	16	17	18	19	20	21
22	23	24	25	26	27	28
29	30	31				

SEPTEMBER

S	M	T	W	T	F	S
		1	2	3	4	5
6	7	8	9	10	11	12
13	14	15	16	17	18	19
20	21	22	23	24	25	26
27	28	29	30			

APRIL

S	M	T	W	T	F	S
			1	2	3	4
5	6	7	8	9	10	11
12	13	14	15	16	17	18
19	20	21	22	23	24	25
26	27	28	29	30		

OCTOBER

S	M	T	W	T	F	S
				1	2	3
4	5	6	7	8	9	10
11	12	13	14	15	16	17
18	19	20	21	22	23	24
25	26	27	28	29	30	31

MAY

S	M	T	W	T	F	S
					1	2
3	4	5	6	7	8	9
10	11	12	13	14	15	16
17	18	19	20	21	22	23
24	25	26	27	28	29	30
31						

NOVEMBER

S	M	T	W	T	F	S
1	2	3	4	5	6	7
8	9	10	11	12	13	14
15	16	17	18	19	20	21
22	23	24	25	26	27	28
29	30					

JUNE

S	M	T	W	T	F	S
	1	2	3	4	5	6
7	8	9	10	11	12	13
14	15	16	17	18	19	20
21	22	23	24	25	26	27
28	29	30				

DECEMBER

S	M	T	W	T	F	S
		1	2	3	4	5
6	7	8	9	10	11	12
13	14	15	16	17	18	19
20	21	22	23	24	25	26
27	28	29	30	31		

CALENDAR

1993

JANUARY

S	M	T	W	T	F	S
					1	2
3	4	5	6	7	8	9
10	11	12	13	14	15	16
17	18	19	20	21	22	23
24	25	26	27	28	29	30
31						

JULY

S	M	T	W	T	F	S
				1	2	3
4	5	6	7	8	9	10
11	12	13	14	15	16	17
18	19	20	21	22	23	24
25	26	27	28	29	30	31

FEBRUARY

S	M	T	W	T	F	S
	1	2	3	4	5	6
7	8	9	10	11	12	13
14	15	16	17	18	19	20
21	22	23	24	25	26	27
28						

AUGUST

S	M	T	W	T	F	S
1	2	3	4	5	6	7
8	9	10	11	12	13	14
15	16	17	18	19	20	21
22	23	24	25	26	27	28
29	30	31				

MARCH

S	M	T	W	T	F	S
	1	2	3	4	5	6
7	8	9	10	11	12	13
14	15	16	17	18	19	20
21	22	23	24	25	26	27
28	29	30	31			

SEPTEMBER

S	M	T	W	T	F	S
			1	2	3	4
5	6	7	8	9	10	11
12	13	14	15	16	17	18
19	20	21	22	23	24	25
26	27	28	29	30		

APRIL

S	M	T	W	T	F	S
				1	2	3
4	5	6	7	8	9	10
11	12	13	14	15	16	17
18	19	20	21	22	23	24
25	26	27	28	29	30	

OCTOBER

S	M	T	W	T	F	S
					1	2
3	4	5	6	7	8	9
10	11	12	13	14	15	16
17	18	19	20	21	22	23
24	25	26	27	28	29	30
31						

MAY

S	M	T	W	T	F	S
						1
2	3	4	5	6	7	8
9	10	11	12	13	14	15
16	17	18	19	20	21	22
23	24	25	26	27	28	29
30	31					

NOVEMBER

S	M	T	W	T	F	S
	1	2	3	4	5	6
7	8	9	10	11	12	13
14	15	16	17	18	19	20
21	22	23	24	25	26	27
28	29	30				

JUNE

S	M	T	W	T	F	S
		1	2	3	4	5
6	7	8	9	10	11	12
13	14	15	16	17	18	19
20	21	22	23	24	25	26
27	28	29	30			

DECEMBER

S	M	T	W	T	F	S
			1	2	3	4
5	6	7	8	9	10	11
12	13	14	15	16	17	18
19	20	21	22	23	24	25
26	27	28	29	30	31	

NOTES